FINDING PEACE

FINDING PEACE

Devotionals for Christians With Anxiety

SARA NESBITT

In The Grey Publishing, LLC

First published by In the Grey Publishing, LLC 2023

First edition

ISBN: 979-8-9886561-0-4

Cover art by Anday Aykut

To my family—
Peter, Mary, and Hannah.
And for the dear friends who have walked and still walk this journey with
me.

Contents

preface

I am a Christian minister with a non-traditional understanding of God. Throughout this book, I use *he* and *she* interchangeably when referring to God. I believe that God has no gender; to refer to God exclusively as one or the other paints God in our image instead of us in God's. Though the early church patriarchs preferred a masculine understanding of God, such a limiting understanding of the divine creator is not universally useful for today's readers and Bible learners. Such is especially true for those whose understanding of a father figure (or a mother figure, for that matter) bears shades of abuse and trauma. For them, the concept of "God as father" or "God as mother" would not feel safe, nurturing, or comforting. Bible readers and learners may also find a non-gendered God more relatable. I began by using no pronouns for God at all, but such wording quickly became tedious and awkward.

To share my theology a little bit further... Though God has no gender, Jesus Christ in his first appearance as God incarnate is male; this is the Jesus revealed in scriptures as God's only begotten son. The word for Spirit in both Hebrew and Greek is a feminine noun, so all references to the Holy Spirit use feminine pronouns. Thus, the Holy Trinity is gender balanced and equal.

acknowledgments

Team work makes the dream work, and nothing is more true than when writing and publishing a book.

First, I want to thank Barbra, my editor, for making my book shine.

Second, my team of beta readers helped find errors in flow and consistency while also giving me their great feedback. To Paul, Amanda, and Beth, thank you so much for the time and attention you gave to helping me.

And lastly, I want to thank my family for all their support and encouragement. From Mary putting up with my typing out the first 1800 words while we were at the beach together to Hannah telling everyone she meets that her mom wrote a book. And a huge thank you to Peter for putting up with my distractability and stress as I brought this dream to reality. I love and appreciate you all.

I

Thoughts on Anxiety

a little background

Anxiety stinks, doesn't it?

If you're reading this book, you are probably someone who is struggling with anxiety *and* is a Christian *and* likely is feeling or have felt guilt and shame about feeling anxiety as a Christian. It's a difficult place to be. I've been there and have friends who visit that anxious, guilty, faith-filled place from time to time.

This was me five years ago. A corporate takeover led to a layoff for my husband, who then decided to fulfill his long-held dream of starting his own business. As his wife, I was completely behind him. As the family bookkeeper, though, I wasn't feeling too sure about not having the income stability we'd enjoyed. That was in July. Two months earlier, my grandmother—my last grandparent—died, just forty-eight hours or so after my husband's friend and mentor did. We'd already been to way too many funerals and memorial services that year—my husband's long-time friend and our senior kitty (mostly my husband's) had already died. Then, in early fall, I lost a significant friendship. Most of this took place in the first six months of the year.

I started developing a tic in my face. My daughters' pediatrician made a comment about it when I took them for their annual checkups that autumn. I'd noticed it, but I had no idea what was causing it. I remember noticing that it was pretty bad as we prepared to go on our family's annual weekend trip in early December, but once we were on the road it was gone, so I figured it had something to do with stress. Others started noticing it, including players on my youth soccer team.

I felt it coming and going and was quite self-conscious about it, but I didn't know how to make it stop or what was causing it.

My feelings were all across the board! I felt like I was literally going crazy. More than a few times, I thought I was going to stroke out. I couldn't get a good night's sleep; my brain would wake up in the middle of the night muddling over worries and concerns. With my prayer-mantra of *You did not create us to have a spirit of fear, but of peace*, I'd find sleep again after a while.

For nearly two years, I had no idea what was going on with me. My anxiety had started in the summer. Around twenty months later, I found out my vibrant, beautiful teen was feeling depressed and had thought about killing herself. That was on a Wednesday. That evening, I was crossing the little two-lane road that separates our church's main parking lot from the church and thought, *If a car hits me, I won't have to feel so overwhelmed anymore*. I had no desire to die and millions of reasons for living, but I just needed a break from so much *feeling*.

It wasn't long—the next day maybe—before I found myself in the office of the Methodist pastor-friend who had confirmed my teen. That was a helpful visit, because eight years of college and graduate school studies to be a family counselor had gone right out the window when my daughter told me with what she'd been struggling.

After Ellen gave me a slew of resources, she commented about the tic in my face. "What's up with that?" she asked me. "Could it be epilepsy?" I answered in the negative. Then she suggested "the A word"—anxiety. I thought it was possible, and for the first time in nearly two years, a little sprout of hope began to bloom in my chest. Finally! There was a name for this crazy feeling I'd been having, and with a name, I could deal with it.

As soon as I got home, I grabbed my abnormal psychology textbook and flipped to the section on anxiety disorders. Every symptom checked off. My friend had also challenged me about the fact I hadn't been to the doctor for a checkup in a while, so I immediately made an appointment for a wellness checkup. On the intake form, I noted that I was struggling with anxiety so I could get a referral for a counselor.

Following that appointment, I began seeing a counselor who happened also to be a Christian. I also began practicing mindfulness and yoga. My goal was to conquer my anxiety without resorting to anxiety-reducing medication. I'd take them if I must, but I wanted to try non-pharmaceutical strategies first.

That was over three years ago. I still practice yoga weekly. My counselor, Doug, and I have terminated my counseling journey. I reclaimed my tool box and filled it with new tools.

Unhelpful Advice from People Trying to be Helpful

As a woman of faith and a minister, I know my Bible. I know all the pithy little "spiritual" sayings, and I'm sure you've heard them, too.

- "Fear not" is in the Bible 365 times, so every day we should remember not to be afraid of anything.
- God doesn't put more on us than we can bear.
- You just need more faith.
- Leave it at the cross and don't take it back.
- Just pray about it more.

These are not helpful for people going through anxiety. I prayed a lot. God and I had many conversations. Never once did I doubt God's love for me or lose my faith. I'm not one of those people who ask, "If God loves me, why am I going through this?" Sometimes, we just go through stuff, and God is much bigger than our junk.

God doesn't put anything bad on us. That's just an idolatry of self-sufficiency, because some people—good, faithful, God-loving people—have to go through much more than they can endure.

"Leave it at the cross and don't take it back" is a favorite saying of my dad's. Anxiety doesn't like being left behind, and no one wants to take it back. We can take our brokenness to the cross, but that doesn't mean healing will come for its being there. The two criminals who were crucified with Jesus were at the cross in their moral brokenness, but they didn't leave alive. They left in death, still condemned thieves. Mary, the mother of Jesus, was at the cross, an emotionally broken wreck. She left, still broken and sorrowful down to her soul.

In addition to these little secular quips cloaked as "spiritual" wisdom, there are ample Bible verses about being strong and courageous and about trusting in God. In fact, these verses present as commands to the reader of the words. Over time, they become almost like new commandments, as ironclad as the Ten Commandments and as inviolable, just more "thou shalts" and "thou shalt nots" to weigh upon people's mortal souls. Those who fling these sayings around in an attempt to bolster themselves ultimately end up layering guilt and shame on top of their anxiety. My heart broke as I watched a friend do this to herself.

In 2018, Hurricane Florence barreled straight toward the Carolina coast with anticipated landfall anywhere between Myrtle Beach, South Carolina and Wilmington, North Carolina. We were living near Wilmington at the time and knew it was going to be bad, so we evacuated to mid-state, staying at my in-laws' house. My anxiety went up at first notice of the storm track, and it didn't return to normal until after we returned home fifteen days later.

Yet, many would criticize me for feeling anxious in light of how truly blessed we were through that time. We had a spacious place to stay that accommodated us and our cats, twenty minutes from my parents' house and minutes from two favorite grocery stores, some shopping centers, and a library. We were near abundant cultural and educational opportunities of which we availed ourselves. We even visited a church and connected with new people, as well as some of my former classmates and a friend from our church at home, as we heard and received challenging messages from the pulpit. I also met a business colleague who lives just three miles from my in-laws. We received blessings galore, but my facial tic was pervasive, and I could barely sleep most nights because of my anxiety.

How's this for some crazy truth? *You can feel anxious and trust in God at the same time. You can acknowledge your blessings and your anxiety as they coexist. The two are not mutually exclusive.*

physiology of anxiety

Just as anxiety and stress are closely related, so too are anxiety and depression. In fact, the Venn diagram of anxiety and depression looks like a boiled egg cut length-wise with the symptoms of anxiety being in the circle made up of the yolk, while the symptoms of depression float in the segment of the egg white.

Both depression and anxiety involve chemicals in the body. With depression, neurotransmitters in the brain get out of balance and create the feelings and symptoms of depression, which in turn, manifest themselves in certain behaviors. Depression starts on the inside and work its way out. With anxiety, events happen, our brains interpret them in certain ways, and then, in response, our bodies produce chemicals that affect us. Anxiety starts on the outside and works its way in. The trick with anxiety is changing how we process those stimuli.

The chemicals our bodies produce when we are anxious are cortisol and adrenaline. These hormones are essential to our safety; they help us respond when we're in danger or threatened. When our brains interpret stimuli as dangerous, whether life-threatening (like a bear charging us) or something that's just mildly alarming (say, a security alarm sounding), our adrenal glands produce cortisol. Anxiety causes our bodies to produce cortisol in excess, which can lead to:

- high blood pressure
- type 2 diabetes
- fatigue
- impaired brain function

- infections

Anxiety makes it difficult to sleep as our thoughts bounce from so-called "crisis" to "catastrophe." This leads to increased cortisol levels, which then makes us feel tired. When we're tired, we tend to be fuzzy-headed and make poor decisions without critical thought or reflection. We are also more likely to stave off the fatigue with food, usually going for the high-energy boost of carbohydrate-laden foods, which can eventually lead to type 2 diabetes. Poor sleep combined with poor nutrition compromises the immune system, leading to a higher risk for contracting infectious diseases.

Our adrenal glands also produce adrenaline in response to anxiety. We're all familiar with adrenaline surges—increased heart rate, rapid breathing, increased blood pressure, and dilated pupils. These are all means by which our bodies prepare to fight or flee. Our bodies cannot sustain this heightened level of excitability without serious health repercussions, most notably to our cardiovascular systems.

The cortisol spikes in high-anxiety situations can cause our brains to go blank to any information or thoughts not necessary to our immediate survival. It was about four months into my anti-anxiety disciplines when Hurricane Florence was on track to hit us and we evacuated. My anxiety level was so high that I could barely think; my brain kept wanting to shut down entirely. Yet, everyone in my home—husband and children alike—were looking to me for guidance and direction. I pushed through it, but it was a nightmare. The memory of that time was bad enough to cause me to go beyond anxiety to PTSD symptoms as we approached the first anniversary of that storm.

In summary, anxiety is a physical response to a cognitive interpretation of stimuli; a response to how we think about what's going on around us. Anxiety is not a lack of faith, a manifestation of a lack of trust in God, or anything at all to be ashamed of. God wants many things for us—our wholeness, our relationship, our devotion. God would never want us to feel guilty or ashamed to be human.

having anxiety in an anxiety-denying culture

Our culture recognizes the presence of mental health issues and the need to treat them, even as it would prefer to deny and avoid uncomfortable topics, such as mental health. In light of this dichotomy, we substitute words for our disorders to make them more socially acceptable. Instead of entertaining the possibility we have depression, we simply say we're "feeling bummed." As opposed to acknowledging our anxiety, we bemoan how "stressed" we are. While stress and anxiety may share some physiological characteristics, they are actually quite different.

I've already talked a little about anxiety and how it affects the body, but now let's talk about stress for a moment. Whereas anxiety is pervasive and chronic, stress is more acute. Sudden, often unpleasant incidents or major life events can cause stress. Whatever causes the stress, there is an endpoint to it.

Studies have shown that weddings, for example, are stress-inducing events in people's lives. Weddings are happy times, but no less stressful for it. We're all familiar with work stresses, such as looming deadlines or performance reviews. We're likely also familiar with family stress, like a family member's sudden illness or injury—or maybe even our own.

Psychologists plot stress on a continuum from distress to eustress (bad stress to good stress). Unless we are dead or unconscious, we always find ourselves somewhere along that spectrum. While it's likely the stress-causing event will change us in some way, it has a specific endpoint.

Just as the type of stress falls along a spectrum from distress to eustress, the severity of stress also lies along a continuum.

Acute stress is sudden and short-lived. Common examples are getting stuck in traffic, giving a speech, or taking an exam. These episodes of acute stress can be beneficial; many people find that the release of stress hormones helps them deal better with the situation.[1] When I was in college, I took advantage of this as I was intentional about waiting until the night before the due date to type papers. The release of stress hormones honed my thinking and my focus.

While acute stress is common and something we can usually handle easily, chronic stress is more pervasive. Chronic stress is caused by being exposed repeatedly to situations that cause the release of stress hormones.[2] Over time, this causes damage to the body.

How we respond to stress is unique to each individual person and is a matter of perception. How one appraises their environment or the event in question determines the presence of stress.[3] For example, a final exam might be extremely stressful for one person, but merely challenging for another. My habit of mindfully procrastinating my paper writing in college worked just fine—so long as it was intentional. The one time I forgot an assignment until the last minute caused me a different type of stress, one that left me feeling more panicked than indomitable.

Anxiety is "defined by persistent, excessive worries that won't go away even in the absence of a stressor."[4] Why, then, do people say they're "stressed" when they are, in fact, feeling anxious? It goes back to our illness-denying society.

In America, we worship the idols of productivity and success, and striving for these idols causes stress. In order to attain them, we have to meet or beat deadlines. By claiming to be "stressed," we look important and successful, like we're striving for something, whereas admitting to our anxiety just makes us look "crazy" or "mentally unstable." Citing "stressed" as to why we're irritable, sleeping poorly, and suffering adverse health effects makes us look better while denying to ourselves and others that we are, in fact, suffering from anxiety.

How we deal with stress is often quite different from how we deal with anxiety. A recent spate of stress-inducing occurrences revealed that my tools for dealing with anxiety are pretty much worthless when dealing with stress. It happened in the middle of the night or, more specifically, in the wee dark hours just before the sky lightens up with the dawn. My to-do list started running through my head, and the combination of the length of that list with the narrowing time frame in which to complete it caused my body to have those all-too-familiar responses: faster heart rate, tight feeling in my chest, and quicker breathing.

I dug out my anxiety-reducing tool of mindfulness. I focused on the feel of the sheets and my breathing and... it didn't work. It was nearly impossible to focus with that list and timetable swirling around in my head. Instead, I thought about a situation my older daughter had been in and fictionalized the outcome to make it more satisfactory. (I'm a writer, so creating scenarios works for me.) This neutralized the acute stress, so although my mind was wide-open active, my autonomic nervous system began to calm down, so I tried my mindfulness trick again and was asleep soon after.

This experience was valuable because it helped me understand the difference between anxiety and stress. Anxiety is pervasive and chronic. It's certainly manageable with the right tools, but likely it is something that its sufferers have to attend to for many years. Stress is acute with a definite beginning and end. While the symptoms of anxiety and stress are similar, their treatments are different, as are the tools used to alleviate their symptoms. In times of non-crisis stress, the best way to ease the stressful feelings is to conquer parts of the task at hand. Getting rid of the event that is causing the stress will get rid of the stress itself.

filling your tool box

Now that I've asserted that faith and anxiety can coexist and briefly highlighted the physiology of anxiety, let's go back to the "tool box" I mentioned back in the first chapter. Your tool box is that collection of strategies and tricks you have developed that helps you deal with your anxiety. Your tool box is unique to you; it won't look exactly like anyone else's. As you discover the tools to put into your tool box, you'll find out how to use them in meaningful ways. Remember, these are *your* tools; don't worry about what others might think of them. The important thing is that they help *you*. I'm going to share with you the tools I have in my tool box; feel free to adapt some of these to your own use and, of course, add your own tools to your box.

Tool #1: Counseling. As someone who studied to be a counselor, I appreciate the value of being the one "on the sofa," so to say. I found out a few sessions in that my counselor is a Christian (an advantage of living in the holes of the Bible Belt), but that's not a requirement for me. It was serendipitous, though, because it's one of the many ways God was a very present part of my anxiety treatment. Some people believe that going to a counselor or therapist means so many different things. They may think you're "crazy" if you're seeking professional mental health care. Others may think your need for counseling indicates a lack of faith. Neither of these is true. The brain is an organ, just like your heart, kidneys, and liver. If you had a problem with any of your parts, you'd seek medical attention for it. The brain is no different.

Tool #2: Yoga. Yoga is physical exercise, help for an aging body, and a way to practice mindfulness in motion. One of our yoga instructors also likes teaching us new (to me) Hindu concepts that have helped me be kinder to myself. *Ahimsa*, for example, means "without harm," and I use this as a reminder not to harm myself with my thinking, which then leads to not harming my children with words when anxiety makes me irritable.

Tool #3: Journaling. Fairly early in my counseling journey, I had improved enough to drop to every-other-week sessions. When I dared to dig deep into my psyche to poke around in its depths and when I had some emotional or psychological breakthroughs, I had to get them out in some way so I could process them. It would have been bad boundaries to email them to Doug, so I journaled them. That got these thoughts, feelings, and reflections out of my head so I could deal with them on my own. Some I shared with Doug, but most I share only with the pages of my journal.

Tool #4: Mindfulness. Mindfulness is being present with yourself in this exact moment. The thing about anxiety is that we're only ever anxious about some unknown future. We may feel shame about events in our past, but we don't feel anxious about them. We are too busy living in the present moment to feel anxiety at that moment. Whatever lies in the future is the cause for anxiety. Practicing mindfulness keeps me in the moment. I read a book to learn about the practice of mindfulness, then I installed an app on my phone to help me meditate. Mindfulness requires practice, and for me, it's as simple as spending time focusing only on my breathing or whatever mundane task in which I'm engaged: feeling, seeing, hearing, smelling, and tasting whatever is around me. Being in the present moment has been a tremendous part of staving off anxiety-inducing thoughts.

Tool #5: Scripture. Scripture is to lift us up and help us learn about God's work in the world. It is abusive to use scripture to beat anyone up, including ourselves. Instead of taking scripture passages to layer additional legalism on myself and make myself the center of my thoughts, I use it to remind myself of what God does, how God loves, and how God protects. By its very nature, anxiety makes us self-centered; I pick out passages to make me be God-centered instead.

Tool #6: Clan. My clan is made up of family, dear friends, and folks in our Sunday morning Bible study group. With them, I can say, "Wow, this week was rough" and "Holy moly, was my anxiety flaring up last night!" They love and accept me just as I am. In fact, it was right after that encounter with my pastor-friend Ellen that my husband and I found this group, and it was exactly what we needed at that point in our lives.

the muck pool

It is often helpful to create mental images or frameworks as we meet challenges of a psychological nature, and one that has helped me navigate this often frustrating journey is "the muck pool." As I went through therapy when I was a young minister, I conceived the concept of the muck pool—and this image has served me well since then, both in my own mental health work and my work as a minister. The muck pool is that place we all have to go through to achieve complete health.

The pool itself is disgusting, filled with all the muck we put into it. We put our past hurts, our insecurities, our psychological issues, and any other junk we have to work through into our muck pool. The muck pool isn't deep, never more than chest high on us. It's long, though, about the length of a football field. On either side of the pool is a dark, deep, impenetrable forest, so going around it isn't an option. A narrow, twelve-inch-wide section of cleared land borders the pool, just wide enough for someone to stand on. The far side of the pool is glorious; a place of brightness and color, fresh air, and happiness. This is the goal of navigating the muck pool—achieving this beautiful place.

We all have to get through our own muck pool. No one can navigate it for us, and no one can carry us through it in order for us to avoid getting covered by our muck. If someone were to try, they would drown and drop us in the process. The special few are willing to walk through the pool with us; very few are able to do this. Counselors are excellent at walking beside us through the pool. Most of the closest people in our lives will stand along the sides, cheering us on and supporting us from there as best they can. Others (those who can't tolerate our muck at all) will become scarce during our journey. It is up to each of us to decide what we wish to do with our relationships with those particular people.

~✻~✻~✻~

It's time to use the tool of Scripture to see the ways God is with us and loving us during our battle with anxiety. I chose these passages to highlight God's goodness and steadfast love, while being intentional about avoiding passages that could place an additional burden of guilt on my readers. Turn the page, and let's get started.

II

Devotionals

day 1

So do not fear, for I am with you; do not be dismayed, for I am your God. I will strengthen you and help you; I will uphold you with my righteous right hand. (Isaiah 41:10)

How is that for a promise? This passage has long been my go-to when I'm facing a difficult or challenging decision.

As our anxious brains bounce around from possibility to possibility, we can rest assured in the knowledge that God is present with us. We can also rest in the knowledge that God himself will give us strength and lift us up. We often expect something like a magical zapping from God. We expect that, if we pray, God will zap our situation with his mighty hand and take all the angst away. So often, though, God works through other people. God works through spiritual and mental health professionals to strengthen and help us. God works through our friends and church family. Sometimes he even works through perfect strangers. It's up to us to see where God is working in our lives.

Dear God, I need your help through my anxiety. Please help me see the people in my life through whom you're working. In Jesus' name, amen.

day 2

I sought the Lord, and he answered me;
he delivered me from all my fears. (Psalm 34:4)

Deliverance from fears and anxieties requires some effort on our part. It's not enough to pray to God. That absolutely needs to be a step, if for no other reason than it is helpful to lay out our anxieties, fears, frustrations, and whatever else might be in the mix to the One who's big enough and loving enough to hear us and accept our anxious selves without judgment. You're never going to hear God say, "My child, if you trusted me more, you wouldn't be anxious," or "You just need more faith."

There are quite a few instances where the Bible speaks about seeking God. Jeremiah says in Jeremiah 29, "If they will seek me with all their heart." Jesus says in Matthew 6, "Seek first God's kingdom and righteousness." For God to deliver us takes more than mere prayer. It takes active seeking. When we actively seek God, we will most assuredly find God.

Seeking God carries with it a risk of discomfort. As Dietrich Bonhoeffer stated:

> "Either I determine the place where I will find God, or I
> let God determine the place where he wants to be found. If
> I am the one who gets to decide where God will be found,
> then I will always find a God there, a God who some way
> or other is the kind of God I am looking for, a God I like, a
> God appropriate to my own nature and personality. But if

God is the One who says where he will be found, then this will very likely be the place that at first does not at all fit my own nature and character, a place I probably will not like at all. This place is the cross of Jesus."[1]

We want to seek and find instant relief. Often, though, we seek and find people God puts in our path, fellow travelers on the road of our life who are willing to walk this journey with us. It is through them that we find surcease from our fears. We find them for ourselves and are those persons for others.

Dear God, help me always to remember to seek after you. Please allow me to find you even in the places that aren't as comfortable for me, knowing that you are already present there. In Jesus' name, amen.

day 3

Search me, God, and know my heart;
test me and know my anxious thoughts. (Psalm 139:23)

Just as we need to search for God, imagine how it feels knowing that God also searches us! It's both awe-inspiring and terror-inducing. The Bible tells us that God knows our innermost beings. God knows all of our anxious thoughts, knows our hearts, and knows us.

Do you know all the stars in the sky? How about the life in the depths of the seas? Of course not. The top scientists in the world don't even have that knowledge. God knows every part of her creation, though, from the deepest depths of the oceans to the farthest reaches of the farthest universe. And God knows you and me, too. God knows us that intimately—much like an attentive parent knows their child.

We'd like to think we can hide part of ourselves from God, that we can duck and dodge when we're feeling less than perfect, maybe hide in a closet or behind a large bush. It doesn't work that way, though. Hiding comes from shame, and when we're wanting to hide from God, God is placing a hand on our heads and saying, "I love you, my child." Then God compels us to raise our eyes to her to hear that beautiful affirmation, "Just the way you are." God wipes out our shame with steadfast, unconditional love and complete acceptance—anxiety and all.

Dear God, thank you so much for caring about me enough to search me and know me. Thank you for loving and accepting me, even with all my less pleasant parts, including my anxiety. Amen.

day 4

I will listen to what God the Lord says;
he promises peace to his people, his faithful servants—
but let them not turn to folly. (Psalm 85:8)

Peace. What does that word mean to you? What do you envision when you hear it? Probably, your visualization of peace varies based on what's going on with you and in the world around you. Many people think of peace as an absence of outer conflict or fighting. How many family members think there's peace within the family because no one is outwardly fighting? Yet, one of my friends said that, in the months before his wife and he divorced, there was no fighting; it was like everyone was walking on eggshells. That doesn't sound very harmonious.

For those of us who were alive between 1950 and 1990, the Cold War era proved that an absence of fighting doesn't necessarily mean peace. While there were conflicts and battles at various points around the world, there was also the threat of outward hostilities. Although Americans on the home front weren't seeing fighting here, just the knowledge of a threat caused heightened tensions.

It is often like that with us, too. We aren't in conflict with anyone, yet we feel decidedly restless and with no sense of peace within ourselves. We have to find that peace. Peace comes from God. At the same time, God gives us ways to declutter our minds and spirits to find that peace. For there to be peace, there must also be silence. In this silence, we can feel God's peace flowing over us.

Dear Lord, please help me silence the voices in my head so that your peace can fill my spirit. In Jesus' name, amen.

day 5

You will keep in perfect peace
those whose minds are steadfast,
because they trust in you. (Isaiah 26:3)

God does this. God is the "you" Isaiah is addressing in this passage. There is a reverse sequence in this passage. First, people trust in God. From that trust, their minds are steadfast. Then, God keeps them in "perfect" (or complete) peace.

What does it take to trust in God? That's a hard one! For believers with trust issues, trusting God doesn't come as easily as it might for other people. Trusting God has to be a daily, constant discipline of choice. We are unable to assume that God will make everything work out, because we don't assume that about anyone. Yet, our faith in, experience of, and love for God likewise make it impossible to doubt God will come through for us. By making trusting in God a daily discipline, much like praying or scripture reading, we see how God is working in our lives and justifying our trust in her.

As we do trust in God, then our minds will become steadfast, the prophet tells us. This means that our minds become unshakable. They attune to God, determine to follow her, and are resolute in their faithfulness toward her. Restless minds cannot hold solidly, though. This is where tools come in.

The practice of mindfulness, when accompanied by the discipline of trusting in God, leads to minds that are steadfast. These minds have determined that God is trustworthy, and through the practice of mindfulness, they have settled their minds in that trust. Their resolution of mind makes it then possible to find peace.

The Hebrew word commonly translated as "perfect" also means "complete." As we attain this complete peace, we shouldn't fool ourselves into thinking that we will always have a calm, stress-free existence—what we might think "perfect peace" looks like. We will have a completely settled frame of mind, and that's what God's peace looks like. It's more the peace of a crying baby in her mother's arms; she may have gas, an empty tummy, or a wet diaper, but she knows all will be well, because she trusts the one who's holding her.

Dear God, help me trust you more. Make my mind steadfast and grant me your peace. In Jesus' name I pray, amen.

day 6

In peace I will lie down and sleep,
for you alone, Lord,
make me dwell in safety. (Psalm 4:8)

Oh, man, who doesn't love a good night's sleep? Yet, when anxiety is overwhelming you and anxious, neurotic thoughts raid your mind, there's just no help for it. You either have trouble going to sleep or you wake up during the night with your mind churning. Then cortisol and adrenaline kick in, and that may as well be the end of it.

Remember, those hormones are our bodies' response to danger or threats, and our minds make us think these external circumstances are threats (sometimes, they legitimately are). We can't sleep in dangerous situations, so we stay awake, aware--or maybe even hyperaware--going over and over all the "what-ifs" we can conjure.

We are able to sleep when we rest in the Lord and the safety that comes from that. When the thoughts begin to creep in, I recite my mantra, *Lord, you created us to have a spirit of peace, not one of fear.* Eventually, this helps me get back to sleep. I often pair that with mindful breathing and focusing on what is around me. I hear the soft whir of the ceiling fan and my husband's breathing, and I focus on the feel of the sheets against my skin and the places where my husband and I are touching.

If we can bring our focus to the present moment where we know we're safe and secure in the protection of the Lord, then we can find the stillness in our minds to go to sleep or go back to sleep. While my mantra isn't straight out of the Bible, it's a synthesis of ideas of what I know God wants for us. God doesn't want us to be fearful, and God does want us to live in the safety and protection only our heavenly parent can provide. When we are securely in that place, then we will find the peacefulness that will return our elusive sleep to us.

Dear Lord, you have created me to have a spirit of peace, not of fear. Please help me find your peace so I may get the rest I need tonight. In Jesus' name, amen.

day 7

Come to me, all you who are weary and burdened, and I will give you rest.
(Matthew 11:28)

Anxiety is such a heavy burden to bear. It weighs down our hearts, our minds, our spirits, and our steps. In fact, everything with which we're supposed to love God becomes buried under this load of worry. That makes it hard to love God, love ourselves, love others, and even to function at all. Carrying our anxiety around is exhausting because of what it is and how it affects us.

Jesus calls to us, though, and invites us to let go of that burden. He invites us—those who are weary and burdened—to come and enter into his rest. I see this verse as instructional for us, as we are on a journey to handle or control our anxiety even as we are also on our Christian journey. When you go on a journey, you don't walk or drive non-stop. Occasionally, you stop to rest, to fuel up either your car or your body, and to grab some sleep. If we stay in one place, we don't continue the journey. Resting in Jesus is wonderful, but if we stay here and rest, we will never learn how to control the anxiety that is trying to take over our lives.

When I started my own anxiety treatments, I began to practice yoga. Yoga requires one to be mindfully in the moment, because it is extremely difficult to concentrate on and hold poses when you're plotting the next day's to-do list, fretting over that meeting you have coming up, or worrying about the parent-teacher conference later in the week. For the seventy-five minutes in the studio, there is nothing for me outside of yoga, except for the recipients of the positive energies I send out. Eventually, though, the singing bowl chimes to signal the end of savasana, we close practice with a round of "Om," and practice is over, signaling the return to the real world.

I imagine that resting in Jesus is very similar to this time. It is an incredible break from the world while we're doing it, much like yoga, but at the same time, it's only a rest stop on the journey. We can remember, however, that Jesus travels with us, so while we might leave the restfulness of yoga, the rest of Jesus stays with us in his presence as we travel.

Dear Lord, thank you for traveling this journey to control my anxiety with me. Thank you for welcoming me to your presence and providing rest for the journey ahead. Amen.

day 8

Pray without ceasing. (1 Thessalonians 5:17)

It would be truly challenging to pray all day, every day. When we think of people kneeling in prayer for hours at a time, we often envision cloistered nuns or monks, not those of us who have lives, children, and jobs. Let's rethink this, though. What, exactly, is prayer?

Imagine going on a weekend trip with a friend. All weekend, your friend doesn't say much to you beyond asking you for things and maybe thanking you after you've done those things. You want to talk to your friend. You have things to say, meaningful, rich, enlightening things to say. All you're hearing, though, is: "Will you hand me the towel? Thank you." Or, "Will you please pass the TV remote? Thank you." There's no conversation, just this constant stream of requests. You want to hear what's going on with your friend, what she's thinking and feeling. At the same time, you want to open up and be transparent with her, with what you're thinking and feeling. Yet, the opportunity never arises.

I imagine God feels like this most of the time. While God wants a relationship with us, we're just inundating him with our requests. Maybe occasionally we remember to show our gratitude. Prayer is a two-way conversation, not merely a barrage of requests. When we pray without ceasing, we not only speak to God, but we are also listening to God. That is prayer—engaging in this two-way conversation. This means that we listen to God as much as we speak to him.

Because we enjoy this open communion with God, we are able to pour our everything out to him. We can express our despair, our fears, and our angst, all to someone who loves us unconditionally and won't judge us for how we're feeling. We tend to think of these emotions as being negative because they don't feel so good. Truth is, emotions are morally neutral; it's what we do with them that brings right and wrong into the equation.

For your prayer today, be intentional about listening for God. God speaks through the Spirit directly to us and sometimes through the Bible, music, other people, and nature. It's just for us to listen.

day 9

Do not be anxious about anything, but in every situation, by prayer and petition,

with thanksgiving, present your requests to God. (Philippians 4:6)

What would happen if we were to move these phrases around a bit? Maybe if we presented our requests to God in every situation, coming to God with prayers of petition and thanksgiving, we would have no reason to be anxious. That would work if anxiety weren't so insidious and sneaky, creeping into our minds and our thoughts before we realize what is happening.

When we initially begin to struggle with anxiety, we are unaware of the triggers that set it off—and there are always triggers. Sometimes, even after we have been treating anxiety for a while, we'll begin to feel the physiological markers of anxiety without even being aware that we're anxious at all.

Then, it's go-to-God time. Through whatever means necessary, She works in and through anxiety treatment. God could work through the spiritual gifts of mental health practitioners, pharmacists, and friends. She works through enabling our bodies to move in certain ways (certainly something for which to feel grateful!). God works through every single tool in our tool box.

We go to God, thanking her for the gifts the Spirit has imparted to all those people who make our anxiety treatment possible, and we pray for discernment. We pray that we will recognize our triggers. We pray that once we do, we are able to pray for God to intercede in our anxious thoughts and responses, stopping them before they have a chance to start. We pray for peace. Maybe this, as a spiritual practice and discipline, will help us not to feel anxious. We cannot, however, discount the ways God is working through others.

Thank you, God, for the ways you use others to help me. Please help me recognize my anxiety triggers so that I will know your intercession in my mind. In Jesus' name, amen.

day 10

No discipline seems pleasant at the time, but painful. Later on, however, it produces a harvest of righteousness and peace for those who have been trained by it. (Hebrews 12:11)

We have taken a look at some of the physical and spiritual practices that are beneficial for treating anxiety. These practices are seldom easy, and it often takes discipline to maintain them. Some nights, I'm comfy at home and don't want to go out to my yoga practice. Sometimes, I would rather skip my counseling session. When I intend to sit and journal my emotions, I grab my book or the TV remote instead.

Spiritual disciplines, especially those that might ultimately benefit my mental health, are so hard to maintain—but maintain them I must. I wish it weren't so. I wish I could say one prayer to God and *poof,* no more anxiety forever and ever, amen. Unfortunately, it doesn't work that way.

There are distinct benefits to maintaining the disciplines required to fill our tool boxes and then to use those tools at the appropriate time. One, with every discipline in which we engage, we grow as people and improve ourselves. Two, the unpleasantness of the discipline that the writer references makes the results that much sweeter. Think of the pain of working out, and also think of the pride that comes with seeing the results. It makes those hours of sore muscles disappear from memory. Three, once we survive the pain of the discipline, we're able to harvest the benefits. In this case, those benefits include peace.

What is peace worth to you? Peace is the reward for exercising the disciplines of prayer, vulnerability, and using your tools. The pain will leave us spiritually and psychologically stronger, but we must have people with us to get us through it. Is that gain worth the pain? I think it is.

Dear God, be with me through the disciplines I need to practice in order to attain the peace I am desperately seeking. In Jesus' name, amen.

day 11

The Lord gives strength to his people;
the Lord blesses his people with peace. (Psalm 29:11)

How amazing it is to know that the Lord gives us the strength we need! This isn't a fallback to that familiar heresy, "God doesn't put more on us than we can bear." Far from it. This is an assurance that God does strengthen us. Sometimes, God may only strengthen us for the next step.

I like to walk for exercise. To celebrate the third anniversary of my total lifestyle change for better health, I decided to complete my first 5K. This wasn't some easily comfortable autumn event with mild, dry temperatures; it ended up being in a tropical environment complete with temperatures in the mid-80s and the requisite high humidity. Though we had an unexpected breeze, nothing changed the fact that this was a tough course. How did I get through it? One step at a time, the *next step* at a time.

This seems obvious. After all, it's impossible to take the next five or ten steps at a single time, let alone the next 1,000 feet or half-mile. We have to tackle the challenge with just the next step. When we begin to look too much at all the steps ahead of us, that is when we feel overwhelmed and begin either to sink into the depths of anxiety and despair or lose heart altogether.

When we focus only on *this* step, it is much easier to see God with us on our journey. When we see God present with us, we also see how God is working on our behalf to strengthen us for what comes next.

That strength from the Lord will get us through this step and give us what we need for the next one. As we are mindfully present to where we are, we are better able to realize God's presence with us.

Almighty God, thank you for giving me strength for each step of my journey. Please keep me focused on you so that I may feel your presence with me. In Jesus' name I pray, amen.

day 12

So don't worry about tomorrow, for tomorrow will bring its own worries. Today's trouble is enough for today. (Matthew 6:34, New Living Translation)

This is one of my favorite verses because it reminds me to stop doing that thing I do that isn't helpful for my life and mental health. Worry is insidious, isn't it? Both big worries and little preoccupations will make us pay more attention to tomorrow than to today. Maybe it's "What will I make for dinner tomorrow night?" or "Is that office-mate sabotaging my project?" One of these leads to some planning and preparation—going to the store or taking something out of the freezer. The other leads to paranoia and panic, which will compromise your performance at work.

Why in the world do we want to add to the worries of today by multiplying them by our imagined troubles of tomorrow? We can only know the worries and troubles of today, and even those we see as though we are looking in a mirror; the image is incomplete, possibly distorted, and from only one perspective. A day may start out with troubles, frustrations, or problems, and at that point, we resign ourselves to having a horrible week instead of seeing God's strength to get us through the next hour.

When we start piling tomorrow's worries on top of today's troubles, we compromise our ability to handle today and what it may bring—both the good and the bad. The compounding effect of the two is overwhelming and paralyzes our ability to think rationally, plan, and execute what we need to do, even if it is something as small and minor as swinging our feet to the floor and getting out of bed. It is foolish to do this, and we know it doesn't benefit us, but we do it anyway. Such is the curse of anxiety.

While we can think, "This is sort of dumb to do and isn't helping things any," at the same time, that part of our brain that is wired to be in crisis mode almost all the time can't help it. It thinks, *If I think about the worst things that can happen, then I'll be ready for them.* This is a lie; we are never ready for them. All too often, those "worst things" never happen, and we have wasted an entire day of our lives worrying over nothing in addition to banking some excess worry for the next day.[1]

As I tell myself, "STOP it already!" Today's troubles are enough to deal with. This hour's troubles are enough to deal with. Chances are, when we live through first this hour, then this hour, then this next hour, all without troubles, then we will eventually learn that not every hour will have troubles. With time, we may even stop looking for them.

God of peace, please guide me through this day, hour by hour. I know and trust that you are already in tomorrow and, therefore, I have nothing to worry about. In Jesus' name, amen.

day 13

Give us today our daily bread. (Matthew 6:11)

It is difficult for our American minds to wrap around this verse. It is a familiar part of the Lord's Prayer, and perhaps we give most of our focus to the words "give" and "bread" as we pray this, requesting that God provides us with the food we need—or want. How often, though, do we focus on "today" and "daily" as we pray this prayer? Do you go out in the morning and secure your food just for that day? In our affluent culture, we wisely take advantage of buy-one-get-one deals and will stock up on cans of vegetables, several boxes of macaroni and cheese, and enough bottles of salad dressing to start our own salad bar. We have spacious pantries and stand-alone freezers to store all our extra food. We do what we can to avoid having to rely on God to give us our "daily" bread.

What if, though, we prayed this line as "Give us today _______?" With what would you fill in that blank? What is it you need just for today? We might fill in that blank with patience, grace, hope, strength, relief from pain, peace, or any of the plethora of gifts from God. Some people may also need to pray for food for the day or gas money, and that's good, too. When we pray to ask God to give us what we need for today, then we are trusting her to give us what we need for today. We aren't worrying about tomorrow or next weekend or next week; it's only about today.

We can pray this prayer requesting God's gifts for today for others, too. When you are in a prayerful state, either actively in a time of prayer or intentionally listening for God's word for your life, the Spirit may place someone on your heart for some reason. You have no idea why, but for some reason, this person comes to mind and won't leave it. That's when you can pray that God will give that person what they need for today; God knows their needs, even if you don't.

Dear God, please give me ___________ for today. (Fill in the blank. Repeat as necessary, listing each and every thing you need for today.) In Jesus' name I pray, amen.

day 14

Immediately, Jesus made his disciples get into the boat and go on ahead of him to Bethsaida while he dismissed the crowd. After leaving them, he went up on a mountainside to pray. (Mark 6:45-46)

The key sentence here is the last one: "After leaving them, he went up on a mountainside to pray." Not even Jesus could be around people twenty-four/seven without taking some time alone to regroup and pray. In our family, we call this "de-peopling time," and it is essential for our emotional health as highly sensitive people (aka empaths). It also helps us recuperate if we have been around people who are giving off negative or toxic vibes, neither of which is beneficial to those suffering from anxiety.

In the passage preceding this one, Jesus has just learned of the death of his cousin, John the Baptizer, and has fed the multitudes, regarding them with "compassion," as the NIV terms it. That is a lot of emotional strain! Can you imagine it? Jesus is grieving the death of his friend and cousin, but he still needs to minister to these followers who were lost, "as sheep without a shepherd."

Being mindful that Jesus was as much human as he was divine, his emotional and psychological needs were the same as those of any minister or teacher or physician. He needed a break to rest and regroup, and he chose to go off by himself and pray to achieve this.

We are no different. It is impossible for us to give of ourselves to our families, jobs, and friends without getting a refill for ourselves. You've heard that "You can't pour from an empty vessel," and that goes for all of us. Now layer anxiety on top of the normal demands on our time and energy. Anxiety drains us of much of our energy as we struggle to have just what we need to survive and function. For us, it means making and taking more time—as much as it takes—to recuperate our physical, emotional, and mental strength.

The best way I have found to accomplish this is to go off by myself. Maybe I don't fall on my knees beside my bed. Often, this looks more like my falling across the bed and savoring the silence. When I am silent, I am better able to hear God speak. In this restorative period, I can allow my mind to rest, and that refreshes me for what comes next. God gives us the choice to rest; it is up to us to choose it.

Dear Lord, thank you for being there in my restful moments. Thank you for allowing me to rest in you. Amen.

day 15

Take my yoke upon you and learn from me, for I am gentle and humble in heart, and you will find rest for your souls. (Matthew 11:29)

"Learn from me," Jesus says. Why? Because of what he is (gentle and humble in heart) and because of what he provides (rest for our souls). For the person suffering from anxiety, there is no automatic rest. There is no relief from mental, emotional, psychological, or spiritual weariness. I remember telling someone one time that I was spiritually exhausted. That woman looked at me like I'd grown horns and a tail and rebuffed my statement with, "How can you be spiritually exhausted if you're a Christian? Just pray for the Spirit to fill you with energy."

"Just pray about it" is the advice people like to give instead of praying *for* you or journeying through the shadow places of the soul with you. The Lord does not call or equip all believers to walk through those dark valleys, but all of us can pray for our wounded siblings in Christ.

Over the past few days, we have reflected on some teachings and examples of Jesus. We can sum those teachings up as "be in the present," and the example as "it's okay to put yourself in timeout and pray." These are two excellent lessons that Jesus gives us and that he reiterates in some form or fashion throughout the gospels.

As we become more and more like Christ through the spiritual disciplines of prayer and studying the scriptures, it will become increasingly easier to follow these practices of Jesus. We will more often find ourselves in the present moment, where we will be better able to see the suffering of humanity around us. We will also be present to ourselves and be able to find that much-needed rest for our souls.

One caveat: We will slip, and that's okay. Sometimes—more often than we want to, in fact—we will stray off the path of following Jesus. When we get back on the path, we will find him waiting for us to catch back up. That's just how God's grace works.

Thank you, God, for sending Jesus to show me how to find rest and peace for my weary soul. Restore my soul, I pray. In Jesus' name, amen.

day 16

The Lord is close to the broken-hearted
and saves those who are crushed in spirit. (Psalm 34:18)

When we are feeling crushed and broken, we often feel all alone. We don't feel like we're "fit company," and if we're honest with ourselves, trying to be fit company (either presentation-wise or personality-wise) just feels like too darn much work. Why go through all the trouble when it's safer to stay holed up at home in our fleece jammies and not inflict our misery on others? Besides, we figure, they won't want us around, anyway, because we're just too... broken. Imperfect. Sad. Anxious.

You may or may not believe this, but God is present to us in those times. God sees us in our unshowered, messy-haired, tear-streaked, freaking out state and barges right into our personal space with her love. We don't see this. When we're steeped in our anxiety or depression, when we are feeling like life has beaten us up and we simply cannot rally enough to fight back, we don't think we're worth being around people, let alone the Creator of the universe.

As the Delphic oracle said (and the Swiss psychiatrist Carl Jung made famous), however, "Bidden or unbidden, God is present." We don't have to feel worthy of her presence for God to save us in the midst of our brokenness. When we are "crushed in spirit," when we are spiritually exhausted and wonder how in the world anyone could ever love us, God steps in to save us.

This happens less as a dramatic, miraculous "zapping" and more through the quiet work of people who care about us. It could be the friend who wonders why you're so quiet on your social media accounts. It could be the boss who notices a dramatic change in your performance at work. Maybe it's that teacher or professor who sees something disturbing in your written work. However God chooses to work in our lives, she will save us as we allow her to.

God, who sees me and saves me, please help me see your saving work in my life. Amen.

day 17

Anxiety weighs down the heart, but a kind word cheers it up. (Proverbs 12:25)

When we feel anxious, our hearts feel heavy. In Chapter 3, I discussed the way anxiety works in our bodies and how the endocrine system releases cortisol and adrenaline in response to our brain interpreting input as threats to our safety. One effect this hormone release has on our bodies is an accelerated heart rate. While our hearts can trip along at their usual rate and we barely notice them, when they are beating faster, we feel their heaviness. Our hearts may also feel leaden as worries weigh on our minds. Anxiety makes us feel inwardly heavy.

Have you ever been in one of those states of anxious despondency and then someone, whether friend or stranger, said just the right thing to you? Maybe they asked you how you were feeling. Perhaps they sat beside you and listened with an empathetic ear. It could also be that they hugged you and assured you that they were willing to walk with you through the muck pool. Whatever they said, how did you feel? Was your heart lightened just a little bit? Even if the feeling didn't last for long, do you remember feeling more peaceful for that period of time? That's the effect kind words have on others. The best example of this I've experienced recently was my husband noticing how much I had on my plate at the time and how stressed I was. Sometimes, just having someone else notice and acknowledge our distress is an act of kindness.

I'd also like to challenge us to be the giver of the kind word, not just the bearer of the anxious, heavy heart. Even when it seems like everything is going wrong, sometimes summoning up that little bit inside of ourselves to give someone a kind word can help alleviate our own internal weight.

Dear God, please help me keep my ears open for the kind words, and speak them through me. In Jesus' name I pray, amen.

day 18

For I am the Lord your God
who takes hold of your right hand
and says to you, Do not fear;
I will help you. (Isaiah 41:13)

Like a loving or kind word from someone makes us feel better when we're suffering from anxiety, the mere presence of a loving, non-judgmental friend also can help. God promises to be that for us. Picture it: We're walking in the darkness of anxiety or depression, and instead of asking us about the quantity of our faith or condemning our suffering, God merely takes our hand and helps us. The beauty of this help, though, is that God doesn't give us what the world might think we need—or even what we think we need. He gives us the help we truly need.

God doesn't just take our hand; he takes our *right* hand. Throughout history, with around ninety percent of the population being right-handed, men typically kept their right hands free to wield their weapons. To have their right hands thus compromised would have left them vulnerable and unable to defend themselves. However, God takes our right hand, telling us that we don't have to worry about defending or protecting ourselves. God has that covered. He will protect and defend us. We can rest in him.

Despite having God's presence with us and his helping us, we are still going to feel afraid, worried, and anxious. God knows this, which is why the prophet says, "Do not fear." God would not have said this if we weren't going to do it. (A good example of this comes from parenting.

Parents of older children never have to tell them not to stick knives in electrical sockets, because the children know better.) God knows we're going to have all the feelings; he created us that way and gave us the capacity to feel a vast array of emotions, after all. God never condemns or punishes us for our emotions. Even when the Bible says "Don't be afraid" repeatedly, at no time does God punish his people for feeling afraid or anxious. Only people judge others' negative emotions. God simply walks beside us, holding our hands, protecting us, and helping us. With that divine presence with us, perhaps it'll help us feel less anxious and less afraid.

Dear God, I thank you for being present with me, even when—especially when—I don't feel you and don't feel worthy of your presence. Please help my fear be lessened as we walk together. In Jesus' name, amen.

day 19

Then they sat on the ground with him for seven days and seven nights. No one said a word to him, because they saw how great his suffering was...

"I have heard many things like these, miserable comforters are you all! Will your long-winded speeches never end? What ails you all that you keep on arguing?"

(Job 2:13; 16:2)

There isn't a moment in which I thought I would ever be including a passage from Job in this book. Job is a tough book to read and deal with, especially in the face of suffering. However, as I wrote about God's nonjudgmental presence with us, I remembered how Job's three friends, before they started pontificating on his supposed "grave sin," did the best thing: They sat with him in silence because they could see how great his suffering was.

When we are suffering in any way, the last thing we want is for someone to come along and ask us what we've done that is so bad to have warranted our agony. This goes double with anxiety and depression, both of which begin in the brain. Yet, if you suffer from either of these, you've probably heard some of the comments I mentioned previously, in addition to admonitions just to "get over it." That isn't helpful at all, and when we have some well-meaning person in our faces saying these things, we just wish they would follow the example of Job's friends early on and sit with us in silence for a while in our suffering—that maybe, just maybe, they'd be God-with-us.

After putting up with his friends' criticisms and judgmental comments, Job is fed up. We can imagine he's also feeling sad, his friends compounding his grief and misery. He calls them "miserable comforters," and look at what he asks them: "What ails you that you keep on arguing?" He correctly identified that his friends' comments were coming from their own place of... fear, perhaps? They feared that, if this most righteous man on Earth could be tormented so horrendously, then they were at risk for similar or worse.

There are a couple of valuable lessons from this passage. We can practice the actions of Job's friends when they were doing it right. When we are with our fellow travelers who are journeying through their own muck pools, we can practice presence and silent empathy. That brings its own healing and is our way of being the incarnational God for them.

We can also remember that fear drives most judgmental comments. Many of us who are suffering really look like we have it all together. We have mastered the fine art of putting on a brave face, bearing down, and gettin' 'er done. We don't have a choice—our families, friends, and employers need that from us. When people around us find out what's happening beneath the surface, they feel afraid. *Holy smokes*, they think. *If someone as "with it" as she feels anxious, what's to keep me from having to suffer from that?* Then they might wonder what we have done to "deserve" the disorder so they can avoid doing those things. At least, that's the hope for them, anyway. We know there is nothing we have done to deserve our anxiety, so we deal with it the best we can.

Dear God, thank you for sending those people to me who are willing to sit in silent presence with me. Help me also be that person for others, too. In Jesus' name I pray, amen.

day 20

But he said to me, "My grace is sufficient for you, for my power is made perfect in weakness." Therefore I will boast all the more gladly about my weaknesses, so that Christ's power may rest on me. That is why, for Christ's sake, I delight in weaknesses, in insults, in hardships, in persecutions, in difficulties. For when I am weak, then I am strong. (II Corinthians 12:9-10)

The apostle Paul had some sort of thorn in his side. We don't know what it was, but it had been afflicting him for three years, and he had prayed to God, begging him to remove it from him. Bible scholars theorize it was some sort of physical ailment, but, again, we're unsure. Whatever it was, it was bothering him enough that he wanted it gone. If you're like me, you have done the same or similar with your anxiety. "God, I don't know why I feel like I'm going crazy, but help me! Please!" That was certainly my prayer many times.

God answered Paul with, "Settle for my grace, because my power is made complete in your weakness." In other words, God didn't promise to remove this affliction, and in fact, didn't remove it. He assured this educated Jewish man that his affliction wasn't the result of some sin he'd committed, that God's grace covered him. But wait! There's more! The Lord tells Paul that his power is made complete in Paul's weakness. In other words, Christ's power isn't revealed in our strength; we have to be weak in order to need and appreciate the power of Christ.

Paul rejoices in his weakness because he knows that, through him, Christ's power will be revealed to those he encounters. The same goes for us. We might pray for healing from our anxiety, but often, the healing comes through others. Additionally, we have no idea how our story of suffering and the journey of our treatment might help someone we encounter.

We have a small Bible study group at church, and as I shared my having anxiety, a few people chimed in: "I have depression," "I'm bipolar," or "I'm a recovering alcoholic." I wasn't the only one who was broken, and my friends' helping me by sharing their journeys was a way that the power of Christ was made complete in our shared weakness and our struggles as individuals loving God and each other in our little segment of community. None of us has experienced the miracle of a divine healing, but we have experienced the miracle of God working in and through us, as well as in and through fellow believers outside our circle, along our journeys.

Dear God, please help me understand and see the purpose behind your not taking my anxiety away from me. Please keep me open to opportunities to use the lessons I've learned through this journey to show compassion and empathy to at least one person I encounter this week. In Jesus' name I pray, amen.

day 21

For the Spirit God gave us does not make us timid, but gives us power, love and self-discipline. (II Timothy 1:7)

"God, you did not give me a spirit of fear." This was my mantra and prayer nearly every night when I'd wake up with anxious thoughts going through my mind. I wasn't sure where this message came from, but I knew it was somewhere in my heart and mind. I'd read this verse, but it had been several years. It was enough, though, to embed itself in my heart and be there in my mind when I needed it.

This verse gives us some key information. First, this Spirit comes directly from God. If she is God-given, therefore, it stands to reason that she is benevolent and empowering. The epistle writer tells us this Spirit gives us power. She gives us power over our fear and anxiety. Jesus refers to the Spirit as "the Comforter," which is one of her functions. Having anxiety in the presence of the Spirit doesn't mean we're lacking in faith or doing something wrong, but we can find a measure of peace knowing that her presence is with us.

The writer next tells us that this Spirit from God gives us love, and the scriptures tell us that perfect love drives away fear. Love from the Holy Spirit is as perfect as love can get. This love also abides with us. Perhaps we need to reflect it back on ourselves during our moments of anxiety. Oh, it's so hard, though, isn't it? When the anxiety dragon has us in its talons, it's nearly impossible to feel worthy of love, let alone to give it—especially to ourselves.

Finally—and this is huge!— the Spirit gives us self-discipline. I want to explore this idea of self-discipline for a moment. The last thing I want to do is to place a "thou shalt" on you or on myself. "Thou shalt have self-discipline because the Spirit gave it to you." No! This self-discipline follows overcoming fear, even if it's for just a moment. It comes after the Spirit has empowered us and given us love to share with ourselves and others. The self-discipline is the last thing, and it takes the most work. By the time we get to this point, though, the Spirit has equipped us to be able to handle it.

This idea of timidity always reminds me of Piglet from A.A. Milne's classic children's books. Even though Piglet is "a very small animal" and often timid and afraid, when it's necessary and his friends need him, he swallows down his fear, finds some scrap of courage (power) in himself, and out of love for his friends, ventures forth after heffalumps, woozles, and whatever other manner of creature is out there. I wonder if we can't show ourselves that same love and, from it, find the courage to track and conquer our own anxiety?

Once we have arrived at the point where we feel like we have some control over our anxiety more than our anxiety is controlling us, once we have bravely faced that dragon through the power of the Holy Spirit, we need to practice self-discipline in order to show ourselves love. That manifests itself in keeping our mental health tools strong and in good working order. We employ self-discipline when we use those tools—journaling, meditation, yoga, and any other anxiety-reducing practices that work for you.

God, thank you for sending your Spirit to dwell within me. Please help me feel her power and grasp hold of it as I remember you did not create me to have a spirit of fear. In Jesus' name I pray, amen.

day 22

There is no fear in love, but perfect love drives out fear, because fear involves punishment.
(I John 4:18a)

In 2013, Disney came out with a movie about two sisters, one of whom has magical ice powers. You might have heard of *Frozen*. Elsa, the older sister, has these powers she knows how to use but not control. At the end of the movie, she learns that love is stronger than fear, and that gives her the clue she needs to learn to control her powers. This verse always reminds me of the moral of this movie: Love is stronger than fear.

If we look at this verse out of context, it looks like there can be no fear if there's love—the love of our family, the love of our friends, or the love of God. In context, this verse is part of a larger passage about the love of God and how we should reflect that love toward others. Yet, you know that you can both feel the love of people around you and still feel anxiety or fear. Why? Because, as the verse says, *perfect* love drives out fear. That perfect love comes only from God—because we flawed humans are not so great at loving perfectly.

If we use I Corinthians 13 as our guide for how we're supposed to love, we fail more times than not. We put conditions on our love; we hold grudges, both big and small; and we sometimes lack patience and kindness. While others' imperfect love is the best they have to offer, sometimes it's not enough to stave off the anxiety dragons.

This perfect love comes only from God, and it's true that, if we're walking in the will of God, we shouldn't fear the punishment John mentions. Our anxiety, though it may feel like a punishment, isn't. We have not committed some grievous sin that has led to these feelings of anxiety. Remember, it's just how the chemicals in our brains react to external stimuli. Let me reiterate: Anxiety isn't a punishment; it's simply something that we have to deal with.

One thing that can mitigate the tortures of anxiety (with its accompanying feelings of going crazy, irritability, and hypersensitivity) is feeling loved. In the first year of my journey with anxiety, I received God's love through Pastor Ellen, a counselor who prayed for me at the end of every session (and, I found out later, outside of our sessions as well), and through our small Bible study group. While my family loved me through the "I'm going crazy!" moments and the psycho-woman screaming, they couldn't even attempt to love me as perfectly as they could until I, then they, understood the intricacies of this dragon living inside me. When we understood that it was the wacky chemistry that was making me unlovable and making it frustratingly hard for me to love them as I wanted to, then we could work together to correct that.

In our small group, feeling the love and support from people who became fast friends was instrumental in progressing through my anxiety journey. We had entered into an environment of shared vulnerability, so there was no judgment. There was nearly perfect love that "keeps no record of wrongs." This—God's perfect love made manifest in imperfect people—is how love drives away anxiety.

Dear God, thank you for the people in my life who love me. Please help me see their examples of love during the dark days of anxious thoughts. In Jesus' name I pray, amen.

day 23

Love is patient, love is kind.
It does not envy, it does not boast, it is not proud.
It does not dishonor others, it is not self-seeking,
it is not easily angered, it keeps no record of wrongs.
Love does not delight in evil but rejoices with the truth.
It always protects, always trusts,
always hopes, always perseveres. (I Corinthians 13:4-7)

A passage on love hardly seems like a good fit in a book about anxiety. However, love is essential to dealing with anxiety; we need to recognize God's love for us, see others' love for us, and learn to love ourselves. The Greeks have nine different words for "love," each one capturing a nuance of that emotion. The one they use in this passage is *agape*, which is unconditional love, such as God's love for us and our love for our spouses. It's the purest type of love.

As we look at this passage, I wonder, *Can we apply this extraordinary love to ourselves?* Can we love ourselves with patience? How about kindness? When we feel like we've accomplished something, that we've conquered our anxiety and aren't feeling it so much but it rears its nasty little head again, can we show ourselves patience and kindness? What would that look like for you? I encourage you to love yourself through patience and kindness when you feel like you're having a setback in the journey of your anxiety treatment.

This passage also says that love is not self-seeking (self-centered) or easily angered. Self-centeredness and irritability are both parts of

"

anxiety. We certainly don't mean to act this way. When we are in the grip of anxiety, we have a hard time thinking about others. We focus only on ourselves because that's truly all we can handle. Feeling anxious makes it nearly impossible to reach out and show love or compassion to others because we are so occupied with our own basic day-to-day survival. Kindness and compassion may be our normal defaults, but the anxiety gets in our way.

Irritability accompanies anxiety. Being in a heightened state of excitability all the time is draining. It leaves us mentally and psychologically exhausted. When you compound that with the restless and disturbed sleep common to anxiety, the fatigue increases exponentially. That type of all-encompassing fatigue makes us short-tempered and impatient with people around us. We need to remember to show ourselves love and compassion in an effort to curb our irritability and self-centeredness. Even if we can't curb it, loving ourselves will motivate us to seek or continue the steps to get better.

Best yet, love keeps no record of wrongdoing. This is when we flip this love from the love we show ourselves to the love that God shows us. Out of God's love for us, God (who is love incarnate) keeps no record of our wrongdoings. We're the ones guilty of doing that. When we have told ourselves that God loves us, so we shouldn't ever feel anxious, we are the ones who feel guilty for having slipped when the anxiety hits. God doesn't hold us accountable for this. In fact, God doesn't even record our anxious, fearful moments. *No record* means no record. God just extends his arms out to us and says, "Get over here! Bring it in!" with one of those huge embraces that promotes feelings of well-being and calmness. If that's God's response to our anxiety, who are we to hold ourselves to any different a standard?

Dear God, you are love, and I thank you for the love you have shown me and the love you have given me to share. Amen.

day 24

Cast all your cares upon the Lord, for he cares for you. (I Peter 5:7)

The Lord cares for you. This is a liberating, refreshing realization. When you're eyebrow-deep in anxiety, it's hard to realize anyone cares for you. In fact, it's hard to believe that you're worthy of that caring. You are, though. Even in the absence of a supportive, nonjudgmental community or network, the Lord's caring is still with us.

This verse instructs us to cast all our cares on the Lord. Please don't read this as something we have to do in order to make our anxiety go away. This shouldn't be another command we need to obey. This verse is an invitation to talk to God in a relational way.

Have you ever had a friend say, "When you need someone to talk to, I'm here for you"? Or maybe you were the friend saying that. What were you communicating? Well, obviously, you were announcing your availability to listen, and you were acknowledging that the other person may not be ready to talk right now. Their readiness in no way impacts your willingness to be available to listen. There's another message that's more implicit than explicit: I care about you. If you didn't care, you wouldn't offer to be a sounding board for your friend.

Another way of thinking about "casting our cares" onto God is to discard them onto God. My mind imagines an overburdened coat butler with his arms laden with the tossed aside coats of guests. God is willing for us to cast our cares onto him in a similar way, only, at the end of the dinner party, we don't have to retrieve them to take with us. In a more relational image, think about when you're with your dearest friend, that person with whom you can bawl your eyes out, laugh, and pour out your heart. The Lord is inviting us to pour our hearts out to her, to unburden ourselves, just as we would with a friend.

God issues us this invitation because she cares for us. That's all. God says to us, "I love you. When you're ready, throw all your mess at me. I'm big enough to handle it. But only when you're ready. In the meantime, I'll be right here, still caring for you, still loving you."

Dear God, thank you for loving me and for being available for when I am ready to give you my cares and burdens. Amen.

day 25

When we can't do it, God's faithfulness can. When we think that our anxiety means we're lacking faithfulness, we can take solace in the fact that God's faithfulness is more than enough.

This passage shows us an example of the maternal attributes of God. She covers us and gives us shelter much like a mother bird with her chicks. The momma bird doesn't care anything about her chicks except for the fact that they're hers. God is like this with us. We are God's creation, God's children, and that is sufficient for her to provide us with cover and refuge.

This verse begins with a bucolic image of maternal protection and nurturing. When birds cover their young with their wings, they give them warmth, dryness, and protection. The psalmist says that there is refuge under God's wings as well. Those wings offer refuge from the elements, enemies, and any other threats. God gives us that refuge, covering us with her wings so we can be safe. In this space, we don't have to worry about the stuff that is coming at us; this is our space of peace and a place to relax for a bit.

In the last line, the language changes. Now the scene moves from pastoral to defensive and looks at a different relational aspect of God. One thing that many Christians with anxiety struggle with is feeling like they're not being faithful to God because of their anxiety. The psalmist tells us that God has that covered, too. When we need protection, God is more than just a mother hen; God's faithfulness is our shield and rampart. Though we may feel like we're lacking in faith, God's faithfulness is more than enough to make up for our lack.

How do we view God's faithfulness? Is it something we get when we put in enough of what we think God wants? For example, if we do enough good works, will God give us faithfulness then? What about if we make church a certain number of Sundays in a year? Or if we share that "I Love God" post on social media? Or do we get God's faithfulness when we ourselves are flashing around our faith? The answer is "no" to all of that. God in her steadfast love gives us her faithfulness and makes that the shield and rampart with which she protects us. That faithfulness is even better protection than a bird's wing; it's iron-clad and rock-solid. God's faithfulness will be there to protect us from all that threatens us, both real and imaginary. That same faithfulness is strong even when ours isn't.

Dear God, thank you for your strong faithfulness and for giving me refuge. Please help me to see your faithfulness even when I feel mine is weak. In Jesus' name I pray, amen.

day 26

"Because he loves me," says the Lord, "I will rescue him;
I will protect him, for he acknowledges my name.
He will call upon me, and I will answer him.
I will be with him in trouble,
I will deliver him and honor him." (Psalm 91:14-15)

What does the Lord require of us? Nothing more than our relationship. The Lord says here, "Because he loves me, I will rescue him." This is not a conditional statement. There's no "If he will love me" or "If he'll obey my commands." The Lord recognizes that this child of his loves him already. Because there is this preexistent relationship where the psalmist not only loves the Lord but also acknowledges his name, the Lord, in turn, rescues and protects him.

This passage is rich with God's promises of protection and deliverance, and it all comes back to relationship. This relationship is reciprocal: Love for rescuing, acknowledgment for protection, a call for a response. The psalmist captures God's unconditional love for us and how the Lord's presence is with us as a side benefit of that love.

As we saw previously in the entry from Job (where his friends sat with him in silence before they began their endless rounds of Job-bashing), here also we see the importance of presence. This isn't the presence of human friends, however. This is the presence of God. God promises to be with us in our troubles. That is reassuring to me, because it confirms what I felt so many times in the height of my undiagnosed anxiety period: God's love and faithfulness are not at all dependent on anything we bring to this relationship.

Many times, I struggled to maintain healthy relationships with the people around me—those I could see, feel, and touch. Though I struggled with my faith during this period, I still loved God and I still would pray daily. A lot of times, I felt like I was praying by rote, but there were many times in there when it wasn't by rote at all. I prayed from the depths of my despairing, frustrated soul. All too often, my prayer was, "I believe. Help me believe more! Please!"

Much of this may sound quite familiar to you. You are likely experiencing something similar right now. You know in your heart that you love God, but you're not feeling like the best example of his child. You have your faith, but it feels weak and shaky. You may even begin to wonder if you're even still worthy of being a beloved child of God. Heck yeah, you are! You are so phenomenally worthy! When your faith is feeling wobbly, God's faithfulness shields you. When you're feeling powerless and vulnerable, God's love is your safety net. When you're feeling like you've moved too far from God's presence, God's presence follows you. God is with us in our troubles—in our worries, stresses, and anxiety. We may not be in the heart-space to feel that presence with us, but it's there.

Dear God, thank you for your presence. When my faith is shaky, please help me feel your faithfulness. When I feel lonely, help me feel your presence. And above all, I love you, Lord. In Jesus' name, amen.

day 27

Many are the plans in a man's heart, but it is the Lord's purpose that prevails. (Proverbs 19:21)

I don't know about you, but "letting go and letting God" is the hardest thing for me to do. I blame it on control freak tendencies and my parents teaching me to take action to make things happen for me. In fact, the two main things that spark my anxiety are feeling out of control and not knowing how things will transpire in the future. This does not stop me, however, from seizing control over whatever I can. When I'm feeling most anxious from feeling the least in control, I go on a cleaning craze or a fitness freak-out; if nothing else, I can control my space and my fitness level. These are my plans, though, These plans help me feel in control, and I like being in control.

God has other plans for my life, though, and these plans tend to trump mine. My best friend once told me, "If you want to know if God has a sense of humor, tell him what your plans are." There's nothing like feeling like the butt of a divine joke! In all seriousness, God's plans and purposes are ultimately for my benefit. The prophet Jeremiah writes, "'I know the plans I have for you,' declares the Lord, 'plans... to give you a hope and a future.'" While my plans give me an immediate sense of control, only God knows what my future holds and can guide me toward decisions that would make my life prosper in the Spirit according to God's will.

I would love to be able to control every aspect of my life, including—especially!—my anxiety. However, being in this much control still does not make my anxiety disappear, nor does it make it easier to manage. Sure, the anxious feelings may dissipate for a little while, but they come back. Still, in the midst of the anxiety and desire for God to liberate me from the anxiety dragon, I prayed for God's will to be done.

Had I not released control over my anxiety to the Lord, I would still be suffering from it instead of managing it. Good things have happened in my life since I realized I have no way to make my anxiety disappear —that this is something I cannot control on my own. The key things have been a renewed appreciation of the blessings in my life and a new realization of all that I am capable of accomplishing. As someone with anxiety, I have suffered the worst I can imagine, though it's not the worst it can be. Once I discovered that I could survive that situation, as horrid as it was, I learned that tackling new, scary challenges isn't all that bad by comparison.

At the end of the day, it is the Lord's purposes that have prevailed in my situation, and they will prevail in yours, too. There is nothing we need to do in order for God to care enough about us to work things out in his time for our best benefit. It is important to keep in mind that God's purposes do not promise beautiful meadows and rainbows. Crap still happens, but God is bigger than any of the mess that enters our lives, including—especially—our anxiety.

Dear God, please help me step back from my own plans and trust that you will fulfill your purposes in my life. In Jesus' name I pray, amen.

day 28

He says, "Be still, and know that I am God." (Psalm 46:10)

Stillness. When you're experiencing anxiety, it's the one thing you yearn for more than almost anything. Maybe you remember what it felt like to be still in your spirit, to have that beautiful calmness in your soul before anxiety became your living companion. Perhaps, on the other hand, you're one of those who can't remember a time when you ever felt peaceful in your spirit. Whichever camp you fall in, there is an undeniable appeal of experiencing that sense of peacefulness and rest in your soul.

God gives us a simple instruction in two parts: First, she instructs us to be still. One way to find this stillness is to meditate, which can take many forms. Some people meditate on scriptures, reading a passage each day and journaling about it. Others practice *lectio devina*, a four-part engagement with the Word of reading, contemplation, prayer, and meditation, all surrounding one verse or passage. Another form of meditation is mindfulness, being present with oneself in the moment. This combines breathing exercises with an awareness of one's body in its physical and spiritual space. However you find stillness in your mind, body, and spirit, do it. By resting our brains in meditation, we enable them to cope better. This will help you get a handle on your anxiety and help you fulfill the second instruction.

God's next instruction is "Know that I am God." All throughout this devotional guide, I have emphasized God as love, presence, comforter, and savior. When we are in a frantic race to escape our anxiety, however, it is nearly impossible to feel her provision of any of these things we need. Like the Ghost of Christmas Present in Charles Dickens's *A Christmas Carol*, God invites us to "Come in and know me better!" However, we cannot know God at all if our minds are busily muddling over "what if" scenarios or worrying about things outside of our control. When we find our stillness, we can also find the space we need to know God better. As we get to know her deeper and more intimately, we are then able to realize all the ways she is with us, especially in the midst of our anxiety. From there comes comfort and peace.

Dear God, please help me find stillness so my mind, heart, and spirit are free to know you in new and deeper ways. In Jesus' name I pray, amen.

day 29

Have you journeyed to the springs of the sea or walked in the recesses of the deep?

Can you bring forth the constellations in their seasons or lead out the Bear with its cubs? (Job 38:16, 32)

The "God of wonders beyond our galaxy" is certainly holy. The Creator has revealed herself in the glories of nature and continues to be actively involved with her creation.

In the early days of our marriage, my husband and I would take weekends and mini-vacations down to the beach, staying at my in-laws' beach house. Their boardwalk went right out over the dunes and to the beach. When we went in December for our annual Christmas kick-off trip, it would often be late before we got down there, 10:00 p.m. or later. The first thing I would do after we unloaded the car was walk out to the end of that boardwalk. That time of year, the beach would be empty, the surrounding houses dark. It would be just God and me out there on the boardwalk. I'd look up at the stars, sparkling like diamonds against the black velvet sky, and I'd think, *The God who placed those stars, who knows each and every one, even those undiscovered by people, knows me.*

Then I'd look out at the inky sea with its lacy white foam kissing the shore and realize that God knows every creature that lives in the oceans, knows every *inch* of those oceans, even the depths unexplored by people. And God knows *me*—inside, outside, the good, the bad, and the ugly. It's a thought that is both exalting and humbling. The God of the universe thinks I'm special enough to know, and at the same time, I'm just an insignificant little speck compared to the entirety of the cosmos.

God knows you, too—inside, outside, the good, the bad, and the ugly. God thinks you're special enough to know, worth the time and energy it takes to know someone and to care about them. This comes from her loving attributes.

We cannot hide our junk from God. So many times when we are struggling with anxiety, we want to hide out. Maybe our church attendance slips, we don't pray as much, or we want to hide from everyone, including God. We feel ashamed to be feeling anxious when we are cognitively aware of all of our material blessings. We feel guilty that we are fighting anxiety when the Bible tells us "Don't be afraid."

God already knows about our anxiety, though. Don't you think that the God who has journeyed to the recesses of the seas has also made a little trek into your heart and mind? The God who brings *Ursa Major* into the night sky at the right time also can bring peace into your dark spirit when the timing is just right.

I encourage you to trust that this God—who is big enough to orchestrate the heavens—is big enough to handle your anxiety. Our God is also small enough to want to be intimately present with you. You can be your broken, messed up, anxious, guilt-ridden, shame-filled self before her. When you come before God with that broken self, with time, something marvelous will happen. You will find healing. It may be through other people, but it will come. Trust the process.

Dear God, thank you for knowing me and loving me, despite my broken-ness. Thank you for providing healing for that brokenness. Amen.

day 30

David also said to Solomon his son, "Be strong and courageous, and do the work. Do not be afraid or discouraged, for the Lord God, my God, is with you." (I Chronicles 28:20a)

Now it's time to "do the work." Dealing with anxiety requires work. At the very least, it necessitates realizing and owning the fact you have anxiety, as well as being willing to name that out loud to a medical or mental health professional in order to start treatment. To that end, it requires a certain amount of courage. We humans don't do well with being vulnerable, but it's in being vulnerable that our greatest healing can begin.

The work also includes tenacity with treatment. Sometimes, treating anxiety flows smoothly and you can feel significant progress. You're feeling incredible and just know that you're going to kick this anxiety to the curb. Other times, it's more like a cha-cha—two steps forward and one step back. The work involves meditating when your schedule is slammed full. It includes making that yoga class when it's cold and rainy outside.

The work may also require digging down deep to dredge up those emotions you've buried and would rather not face, just to vomit them out onto journal pages for the sole purpose of getting them out of your body and in front of you to deal with them. I was dealing with this one time on the beach, and my journal entry begins with descriptions of the waves, the breeze, and seagulls—because I was avoiding the emotional muck. I eventually got to it, but it took a while.

Dealing with anxiety can be discouraging at many times. In those times when your recovery looks more like a cha-cha, it's easy to feel like you don't have the handle on it you thought you did. When something triggers a PTSD-type reaction, you feel like a failure. Every time I feel my facial tic return for no discernible reason, I sigh with a mix of frustration and discouragement, especially when it's been absent for weeks. A little fear and discouragement is normal and even expected.

However, because the Lord our God is with us, we can shelve those feelings in the "God compartment" and get back to our work. I read this verse as a complete symphony of phrases and clauses: Do the work. Don't stop when you're feeling afraid or discouraged. God is with you through the work and the feelings that often accompany a long therapeutic journey.

Dear Lord, you are always with me, even in the dark times of fear and discouragement. Please help me keep on with the work ahead of me when those dark times come. In Jesus' name I pray, amen.

day 31

Now may the Lord of peace himself give you peace at all times and in every way. The Lord be with all of you. (2 Thessalonians 3:16)

This is my prayer for you, for me, and for all who suffer from anxiety. This peace does not come from anything we do or anything we're capable of doing. This peace comes from the Lord of peace himself. Why does God want to give us peace? Because he loves us with a steadfast, unconditional love. How does God give us peace? The Lord gives us peace often through the intercession of others. As you go about the work of getting control over your anxiety, people will step in your way to help you. These people might be friends or family members. They may also be people you didn't know at all before your anxiety diagnosis, but now you can't imagine navigating this journey without them. They're those cheerleaders standing beside your muck pool as you wade across it.

As we look for God's peace, it will help to be aware of every way in which the Lord can give us her peace. We often have a tendency to want the peace to come upon us as if magically poured out on us or through a zap to the back of our heads. All too often, though, that peace comes through ways we hadn't even imagined. It comes when we follow an urge to go someplace that is away from our normal paths—and experience a sense of peace in the place we end up. It comes through the skills we cultivate and practice—yoga, mindfulness, or meditation; or, for some, through prayer, art, or music. Sometimes it comes through the mere presence of a dear friend and spending time with that person.

When we look for the Lord's peace to come to us in unexpected ways, we will most surely find it.

Paul expresses in this verse, "The Lord be with all of you." There's no exact translation for "be"; we might also read this as "The Lord *is* with all of you." The first implies a blessing with a future context; the latter implies an ongoing blessing and an affirmation of God's continuing presence with us as much as with the church at Thessalonica. Just as she was with the church then, God is with us today. "Bidden or not bidden, God is present." May you feel that presence with you.

Dear God, thank you for being present with me. Thank you for providing me with your peace. Amen.

bonus passage

Because of the Lord's great love we are not consumed,
for his compassions never fail.
They are new every morning;
great is your faithfulness. (Lamentations 3:22-23)

There is a hymn in the Baptist hymnal entitled "Great is Thy Faithfulness." If you're unfamiliar with this hymn, which is based on the above verses, here are the lyrics to the first two stanzas:

Great is thy faithfulness, O God my Father,
There is no shadow of turning with thee.
Thou changes not. Thy compassions, they fail not.
As thou hast been, thou forever wilt be.
Chorus:
Great is thy faithfulness! Great is thy faithfulness!
Morning by morning, new mercies I see.
All I have needed, thy hand hath provided.
Great is thy faithfulness, Lord unto me.
Summer and winter, and springtime and harvest.
Sun, moon, and stars in their courses above.
Join with all nature in manifold witness
To thy great faithfulness, mercy, and love.
Chorus.[1]

God's mercy and compassion are new every morning. That means that every night when we go to bed, plagued by anxiety and wracked by the guilt that often accompanies it, the next morning brings God's new mercies. This means that each day God gives us a fresh, new beginning. We may still wake up with anxiety and the feelings that come with it, but God is still compassionate and faithful. Day by day, morning by morning, God gives us a fresh start.

Over time, those mornings become seasons. After waking up to God's mercies each and every morning, we eventually can look back and see how God's mercies greeted us every day throughout seasons, and we can see God's involvement in every season of our lives. This includes the calendar seasons, but also our own personal seasons—seasons of anxiety, seasons of grief, seasons of joy, and so forth. God is faithful to us and is faithful with his compassion, and this faithfulness never changes; it is part of God's immutable nature.

God, thank you for your mercy and compassion. Thank you for being faithful to me each and every day. Amen.

end notes

Chapter 2

1. Humanstress.ca. n.d. *Acute Vs. Chronic Stress – CESH / CSHS*. [online] Available at: <https://humanstress.ca/stress/understand-your-stress/acute-vs-chronic-stress/> [Accessed 9 May 2020].
2. Ibid.
3. Lazarus, R. S. "Psychological stress and the coping process," 1966.
4. https://www.apa.org. 2019. *What's The Difference Between Stress And Anxiety?* [online] Available at: <https://www.apa.org/topics/stress-anxiety-difference> [Accessed 9 May 2020].

Day 2

1. Bonhoeffer, Dietrich. *Reflections on the Bible: Human Word and Word of God.* Translated by Manfred Weber. Peabody, MA: Hendrickson Publishers, 2017.

Day 12

1. A study at Cornell University asked participants to name the things they most worried would happen. The researchers found that 85% of what the participants worried about never happened. Of the 15% that did happen, 79% of the subjects discovered they could handle the situation better than expected or learn from it. Goeway, Don J. *85 percent of what we worry about never happens.* 6 December 2019. huffpost.com/entry/85-of-what-we-worry-about_b_8028368. [Accessed 9 May 2020.]

Bonus

1. Chisholm, Thomas O. "Great Is Thy Faithfulness." 1923. *The Baptist Hymnal.* Nashville, TN: Convention Press, 1991.

afterward

I finished the first draft of this book in February 2020, the same week my counselor Doug and I organically terminated my counseling sessions. I'd progressed, and we were done. Two weeks later marked the beginning of what we jokingly referred to at the time as "the longest spring break ever." It was while my older daughter was on spring break from her dual enrollment courses at the local community college that the world came to a screeching halt due to the COVID-19 pandemic.

The ensuing weeks and months tested my anxiety-fighting tools and my resilience. I suddenly found myself in the simultaneous roles of mom, teacher, college tutor, and crisis-intervention worker, all while feeling very much in crisis myself. I cried—a lot. I wept with my younger daughter when her favorite summer activity was canceled. (She later said it was a good thing because it created the circumstances that led to her meeting her best friend the following summer.) These were not easy times for anyone.

I spent the summer learning about freelance writing, having this book edited, and looking for an artist to do the cover. I leaned on my friends, albeit via Zoom, emails, and text messages. I dug deep into my anxiety-busting toolbox to keep myself going. Along with the rest of the world, I was in crisis but had to plow through it for the sake of my family, especially my daughters. Every day felt like a day of mental health survival. That's why this book, completely edited and technically ready to print, languished in my cloud storage for three years. Until now.

about the author

Sara Nesbitt lived most of her life in a metro area in central North Carolina before escaping to a small town near Wilmington, NC, where she lives with her family and three cats. She holds graduate degrees in counseling and theology and has first-hand knowledge of the struggles that come with anxiety. *Finding Peace* is her first book.